Teaching Haile Selassie to Swim

Family Myths and Legends

Teaching Haile Selassie to Swim

Family Myths and Legends

by

Various Artists

First published 2024 by The Hedgehog Poetry Press

Published in the UK by
The Hedgehog Poetry Press
Coppack House, 5
Churchill Avenue
Clevedon
BS21 6QW

www.hedgehogpress.co.uk

9 8 7 6 5 4 3 2 1

A CIP Catalogue record for this book is available from the British Library.

ISBN: 978-1-916830-38-7

"April always has me thinking about my Grandad, and the fact that he was a great teller of stories. When we were kids he would always come out with these brilliant tales from the War and before, and they have always stuck with me. As I have gotten older some of them became legends and perhaps myths, sitting in my mind, and it has always struck me that there is a part to be played in families and societies for such things.

The one he told that I always remember, was about the time he went on a daytrip to Weston-super-Mare, and taught the Ethiopian Messiah, Haile Selassie, to swim.

Which to be fair is quite a claim and I'm not sure that I ever really believed it.

But yes, my Grandad was from Birmingham and even when I was a kid a day trip to Weston was the focal point of Summer, but...

Haile Selassie in the swimming pool in Weston S&M?

Really?"

MD, April 2024

Contents

Oz Hardwick 11

Phil Santus 13

Ceinwen E Cariad Haydon 14

GP Hyde 15

Kate Young 16

Neil Windsor 18

Mick Yates 19

Rebecca Lacey 21

A C Clarke 22

Felice Hardy 24

Wendy Goulstone 25

Patricia M Osborne 27

Elizabeth Horrocks 28

Liz Kendall 29

Kate Copeland 31

OZ HARDWICK

Turned Out Nice Again

I'm told my father's father tuned George Formby's banjolele, while my mother's brother flew Churchill's delegation to Buchenwald after the War. Though both are uncorroborated, there are photos of the former with the Ardwick Empire Orchestra, and the latter (MBE) standing proud by his plane, and there are verifiable accounts of moonlight jazz and midnight raids, of bawdy songs and roaring motors, a long, long way from home.

I'm sad I couldn't speak to them, though I never has a chance, but I wore my uncle's coat until it fell to rags, and I scraped at granddad's violin until it woke the unlikely dead.

And there was George and Winston, on a bench by Camber Sands, singing songs of the old days and smoking fat cigars. *We remember 'em, yes*, they both agreed when I showed them the family snaps, *and their brothers and sisters, and all the others – we remember every one.*

And I'd like to say I heard a fiddle flying out across the sea, but all I heard were rumours of engines and, after that:

PHIL SANTUS

Yuri

They say that everyone remembers where they were when JFK was shot. Well, no, I was eleven years old - perhaps I was playing footie, in the street with my mates.

I was at work when I heard that another John had been assassinated. This time, I was upset. I still loved the man and his music, despite his unashamed hypocrisy.

On the day of the Twin Towers attack, I noticed a group of engineers huddled around a TV. I walked over to get them back to work, but the look of shock and astonishment on their faces deterred me - and I joined them for a while.

I remember watching the first moon landing on the TV in my parents' living room - a wondrous occasion. It's a shame that Neil fluffed his 'one small step for a man' line, which he always denied. He was a man of action, not a narrator.

Before any of these, I watched the first man into space go past in an open-top car. Yuri's tour took him close by our school, so the children lined the road to cheer, and we waved our Union Jacks. I remember him in his military uniform as a smiling, round-faced man. He waved back to us.

My wife once asked me if I would like to have been an astronaut in another life. No, I said, I am scared of heights and suffer motion sickness in the car. I could never have been an astronaut - I'll leave such heroics to others.

CEINWEN E CARIAD HAYDON

Too Late to Rewrite the History

My Dad told the tale; when I was small
that made it utterly true. Leicester
to Merthyr was a long ride, wee stops
notwithstanding. Eight hours from

leaving home we'd drive through
the final valleys to my grandparents'
warm, terraced abode. Back then, Dad
would stop the car nearby, and point

up to a ruined cottage, precariously
sited by the top of a sagging slag heap.
There it is, he'd say, his voice hoarse,
that's where a bloody handprint

*stains the walls; it will never wash
away. That's where a man was killed,
murdered, murdered for his own
bad faith.* Years later, I yearned

to be told more. Dad refused,
and said I was mistaken, muddled
in the head. Then, on his death bed,
he said, *Sorry son, I misled you. Lied.*

*I saw the palm-mark in childhood; it
drove me wild. I know what I saw; and
I knew this sight must never invade
your clear eyes or haunt your fresh mind.*

My Dad badly misjudged, his caution
lit an unquenchable, dreadful fire.
Today, in nightmared dreams   the hand
comes for my throat. One day

I fear I'll choke and then expire;
my left hand dye-printed on a wall.

GP HYDE

A Life at Sea

My Uncle Bill would spin us a yarn, how they signed him up
as a young deckhand, a deckie as they were known.
They took him onboard at the Royal Dock near Grimsby Town
and put to sea where for thirty years he battled the waves
off the Dogger Bank and told us of storms and gales
that rose up high and threatened to roll his trawler over.

When he became ill, he took my hand and shared
his wish to be buried at sea, to be reunited
with all the mates that he had lost over the years.

'I have made burials at sea before,' said the funeral man
in his long black coat and sober tie. 'We'll drive him up to Tynemouth,
find a skipper and boat to take him
out to the official burying ground.'

The cost was huge, we settled for a simple service at the crem
but I felt bad to deny Uncle Bill his final wish.
At the wake, I chatted to this old guy and said
it was sad his wishes had not been met,
an old trawlerman not laid to rest in the ocean waves.
He roared with laughter, said that
Bill had been to sea for a month at best.
Seasickness had got the better of him
and he'd spent his life as a clerk
in Grimsby's Fish Market by the Royal Dock.

KATE YOUNG

Myth and Memory from Stranraer

Great Aunt Stella was legendary,
a colossus in a tiny frame wired
with muscle and sinew, immune
to the haar rolling off Loch Ryan.

A wearisome journey,
heather threaded through hills,
the roar of the engine
brakes ghosting the cliff.

The ivory house was formidable,
perched on the edge like a gull,
its glassy eyes ever watchful
searching the seas for sassenach.

A green canvas tent
that reeked of stagnant peat
pitched in the nearby field,
eyes excited by moonlight.

Early doors we were allowed inside
the walls adorned with stags' horns,
an ornate dresser crested in wax
and silverware, hallmarks overworn.

A mop of thistledown hair
that framed her wisdom,
facets of amethyst
sharp with the fizz of life.

The housemaid bustled and scuttled
from scullery to parlour like a spider
that knew every cranny, having spun
her web through the manse for eons.

A week of freedom exploring the town
our ancestors' names engraved
in plaques, a clock that hung outside
the kirk, its face flushed with pride.

The telegram arrived in September,
a brutal murder, her amethyst eyes
caved into her skull, a spider found
curled to the curve of her spine.

NEIL WINDSOR

Sir Humbert Heads South.

The intrepid explorer Sir Humbert Snicket - Ginnel
Is a distant Great Uncle of mine
In fact he's so far removed
We haven't seen him for some considerable time

He left to discover The Unknown
The bits where no one else has been
The last contact we had with him
Was a postcard from Milton Keynes

It was one of those risqué cartoon ones
It said the natives were friendly enough
Happy to share what they have
Although ignorant in the ways of The North

Sir Humbert reckons a missionary party should be sent
To educate the heathen Southern masses
On how to eat tripe, breed Whippets
And sup ale from dimple pint glasses

Distinctively rotund
Ruggedly fit for purpose and sound
A descriptive metaphor for Northerners
If one were needed to be found

Sir Humbert then continued his travels
To lands much further afield
Searching for the holy grail of discoveries
But ultimately his fate was self sealed

After embracing technology and going electric
The last time he was seen alive
Was after he ran out of charge in the middle lane
Whilst crawling clockwise on the M25.

MICK YATES

aira force

it is an ideal walk

on a warm sunny day

in the early spring

there are other visitors there

from elsewhere in the country

but their presence does not detract

from the simple pleasure

that this walk can bring

later we lunch by the lake

on the shore of ullswater

amidst the famous wordsworth daffodils

a simple picnic but joyous

i skim stones across the water

and in the distance

glenridding and the other fells

loom in a prussian blue haze

the perfect backdrop

to a glorious day

REBECCA LACEY

Not Yet Three

Not yet three and still in a nappy
damp terry towelling chafing my bud soft skin,
my mother lays out an unworn dress
pale blue , white flowers , puffed sleeves
my big girl pants alongside.

Today we are going for tea
to my mum's new friend
Cynthia
to play with her little boy
Julian
same age as my big brother, it seems,
while the husband is overseas-
most importantly , so the story goes ,
I am to tell her when I need a wee.

The house is big and fancy
and the boys run off to play,
while I am glued to my mum's leg.
She laughs full throated head thrown back -
there must be something in the tea-
I tug at her capri pants ,
-the shine of her black pumps
super glossy like a slide-
Not now , she says , *Go and play*

The boys are nowhere to be seen
so I get up on the sofa,
and feeling a little sleepy ,
settle soft into the cushion .

And this is how the infamous story of me
weeing on John Lennon's sofa is told.

A C CLARKE

Romance

My father saw my mother across a crowded room.
At least that's how he told it.
Said to his friend
that's the girl I'm going to marry.

Her name? I don't know yet.
Let's just suppose it happened,
that some celestial novelist sketched out
the whole scenario while my mother

lectured her dolls' classroom in twenties Maidstone,
my father bickered with his older sisters
three hundred miles away.
I wouldn't go so far

as saying this omniscient narrator
staged World War Two to get those two together
but it was certainly just as effective
as any plot device.

They didn't stop to think.
Was I planned from the start
or did the author slip me in
to up the drama quotient,

having my father see me first three years
after I met the world head-on in black-out,
a war child, born in winter, seas away
from where he soldiered?

Was I an afterthought
given that a half-brother from an affair
was written into the script before I came -
though this promising line of narrative

was never followed up?
The writer got diverted
into the choppy waters of the marriage.
Perhaps that was the problem.

I never knew my role.
It seemed to have been written
for someone else.
My parents never seemed quite sure of theirs.

When it imploded – surely that much was sketched
into the plotline from the start –
the book was closed for good,
three characters escaping from their author.

FELICE HARDY

Family Fairy Tales

My father showed me a photograph,
the image worn and tattered
but the girl was young,
her hair swept back in jewelled combs
and she wore a fine lace dress.

He said it was his mother,
the daughter of a violinist
who played in the Imperial court.
I met the woman in her later years,
my grandmother who lived by the river.

She believed in superstitions
from her old European origins.
Avoid whistling indoors, she said
or you'll invite the devil in,
never place a bag on the floor.

Don't sit at the corner of a table,
or greet me through an open door.
Don't twist your face in that ugly way,
if the wind changes
it will stay like that forever.

When words of wisdom come to my mind
can they be traced to her?
Some of them might not be true,
like my father's story
plucked from his imagination.

WENDY GOULSTONE

Bath Day

Tell us about when you were little, Mum.

'My mother never had much chance to sit down
with us nine children squabbling, the lads fighting
and the little ones squawking to be fed.
On Monday wash days she kept the fire going
under the copper in the back kitchen
to keep the water hot, and, after we'd had our tea,
bread and jam or, more often, toast and dripping,
 she would take the tin tub off the hook
in the back kitchen, put it in front of the kitchen fire
and fill it with the washing water from the copper.
I was the oldest, so always had the first wash,
but you can imagine the colour of the water
after a few dirty knees had been in it.
Then she would get her clothes pegs and hang us
by our hair on the clothes line in the yard to dry.'

PATRICIA M OSBORNE

The Mersey Tunnel

when I was six

a mammoth snake
swallowed me whole

my little legs raced through
its innards to find a way home

engines vroomed one by one
I huddled close to the reptile's spine

lanterns blinked piercing
the dark with eerie green

a monster machine screamed a siren
as it roared past   cloaking me in its shadow

I rattled at the side as the giant contraption
beamed bright lights into my eyes

once it had gone I hurried along
finally reaching the snake's wide mouth

the hissing serpent spat me out whole

*This poem was inspired by a conversation I had with my nanna more than sixty years ago
when I told her that I'd walked through the Mersey Tunnel. Unfortunately she didn't believe
me. I can't think why!*

ELIZABETH HORROCKS

The Journey

They were a large family – a great pack of boys
and one only daughter in the rambling stone house
next to the cathedral, not far from the sea
which they worked, restoring, skilled users of stone.

In the months after Christmas, they woke in the cold
of various Saturdays, and, fuelled well with food
(prepared by the women before the dark dawn)
they followed their love of the oval ball game –
the crush of the crowd, the hwyl and the songs;
men poured from the valleys, the mines and the iron works.
They walked long to join them from their home in the west.
In the dawning they walked – sixteen miles, seventeen hills –
St Davids to Haverfordwest where they found
an easier path: the iron road, the railway,
Crowded in third class they travelled to Swansea
that "ugly, lovely town" to join the great swell,
to cheer or to weep at their proud nation's plight.

Then back, sunk in gloom or buoyed by success,
drinking to drown sorrow or to celebrate a win.
Then the long walk returning in the dark of the night.
Late arrival at home, more food, then to bed...

to wake in the morning in time for the choir.

LIZ KENDALL

Strange bedfellows (use your toothbrush, alright?)

Travel cheap, travel light, stay a week, stay one night,
but to keep your smile bright use your toothbrush, alright?

Dad had taken half of a twin room, nothing grand;
put his pyjamas out, his book on the nightstand,
his toothbrush in the bathroom where it ought to be,
then went out for the evening, to see the city.

Returning from fresh pavements under his feet,
from a couple of drinks and smokes, something to eat,
a giant had occupied the other bed
and with Dad's toothbrush scrubbed at the teeth in his head.

This new fellow looked darkly from over his fist
as it moved back and forth, and Dad picked up the gist
that not being as brawny nor nearly so tall
his best action would be to do nothing at all.

But with Dad's toothbrush back in its place, though unclean,
Dad strolled into the bathroom; took care to be seen;
and then smiling quite kindly at his new-found chum
used the same precious toothbrush to clean round his bum.

He gave a good scrubbing, did not miss a cranny;
his face showed he thought his room-mate quite uncanny
for using so strangely this common device,
as a bottom-cleaner in one's mouth is not nice.

In silence they slept and in silence they woke,
they did not share their names or exchange song or joke,
but never forgotten by either, or me,
was this lesson: that men must live in harmony.

Travel cheap, travel light, stay a week, stay one night,
but to keep your smile bright use your toothbrush, alright?

KATE COPELAND

Dear Nenne,

Just leaving this in the garden, birds
will bring it, up, to you. Shaping some
memories, sensing your arms always
gave me warmth; still aware of sound-
ness, when seeing you in snapshots.
Family album-memory lane, just now,
and then.
Enormous safe-hugs, bosom-warmth;
your way to clutch me down stairs
(you did not quite fit the stairwell).
Legend tells,
you were always that protective of
the yours. Your sister's sons, and you
at the playfield with a potato peeler.
No harm done.
Your husband's caravan, you around
with chocolate creams, kicking his
shins so he'd refuse.
No money then.
Your cloak room's job, at a pleasure
place; story states you were brutally
gentle with the girls. No man dared.
I can imagine this,
growing up in port city must have
been tough, exciting too. You had
a parakeet and knitted winter socks
with nan,
eating custard cake.
Just touching heaven's base, for now,
all well here at castle town. Sending
you a snug-hug back, no sound-
ness ever felt so never-ending.

Love, Katey